CASTLES

of Cornwa

Isles of S

Pete London

Introduction

Castles capture everyone's imagination. For adults perhaps it's the history of times gone by, the grand architecture, or stories of their builders and occupiers. Children can picture knights and princesses, an evil sheriff, bloody gruesome dungeons. Cornwall is rich in castles; their ruins tell us much about our past, and are often set amid breathtaking countryside.

A castle is a purpose-built fortification, sited for defence or domination of its surrounding area; a practical military bastion rather than, say, a fortified manor house unable to resist a determined invader. Cornwall's first strongholds appeared during the Neolithic period, between five and six thousand years ago, as the hunter-gatherer existence gradually gave way to permanent settlements, animal husbandry and crop farming. Several large defensive hilltop or tor enclosures were constructed, shielded by great banks of stone.

Hillforts and cliff castles followed during the Iron Age, and then a long interval occurred before the Normans arrived in Cornwall, building castles to control territory and keep order. Amid frequent political instability, by the late thirteenth century Cornwall's castles had been refined, early wooden structures replaced by towering stone. Tudor times brought new castles with a different purpose; defence against enemies from overseas. During the mid-seventeenth century Cornwall's strongholds played a part in the Civil War between King Charles I and Parliament. By then though, castle-building was at the end of its time; increasingly efficient gunpowder and cannon had emerged, and even the toughest castles couldn't withstand the new weapons.

For further information of all the titles in this series please visit:-
www.tormark.co.uk

Published by Tor Mark, United Downs Ind Est, St Day, Redruth, Cornwall TR16 5HY

This reprint 2014
First published 2011

ISBN 978 085025 427 3

Designed by Alix Wood, www.alixwood.co.uk

Printed by R Booth Ltd, The Praze, Penryn, Cornwall TR10 8AA

Tor Enclosures, Hillforts and Cliff Castles

The best-known Cornish Neolithic tor enclosure is situated on Carn Brea, the huge granite hill bearing over Redruth. Among the natural outcrops, great banks of rock were constructed to defend its three summits, linked by two stone ramparts on the north side enclosing a sizeable space. The encircling rocks and ramparts can still be made out. Carn Brae was the scene of a pitched battle in which its defenders were overrun, and after a period abandoned was reoccupied during the Iron Age.

Bodmin Moor hosts several similar tor enclosures. At Helman Tor, between Bodmin and Lostwithiel, low walls survive as well as several roughly-levelled areas forming terraces; current thinking is that these may have been bases for buildings, perhaps wooden since there's no evidence of stone construction. Rough Tor features several stone walls linking natural rock formations to form a defendable area, and numerous terraces. At Stowe's Pound, on an outcrop near Minions, are two great granite enclosures and many levelled areas, together with a useful marker for the site: the rocky natural phenomenon known as the Cheesewring. Cornwall's earliest castles were constructed by local chieftains and provided refuges during periods of conflict, but they may also have been used as meeting-places, for trading, or ceremonially.

Hillforts and cliff castles from the Iron Age have also left their mark on the Cornish landscape. Of the hillforts, among the most impressive is Chûn Castle near Morvah in West Penwith, built during the third century BC. Chûn is a circular walled stronghold of around 280 feet in diameter, surrounded by ditches and built of granite rather than the usual earthworks. From its imposing hill Chûn dominates the area, with marvellous outlooks over the Atlantic and toward Mount's Bay. Today, much survives: the offset entrance and remains of two thick defensive walls, the inner once perhaps twenty feet tall; vestiges of rooms, huts or perhaps houses; the vital well which ensured water supply. Within its walls too is evidence of a tin-smelting furnace; it's likely Chûn was built to defend the local tin workings from incursions by Irish or Viking raiders. In times of trouble the castle would also have protected the people of three nearby villages.

But Chûn is dwarfed by Castle-an-Dinas near St Columb Major, defended by three huge concentric stone-and-earth ramparts and ditches; all told, the site covers some twenty acres. At seven hundred feet above sea level Castle-an-Dinas has panoramic views to both north and south coasts, a vantage point that has to be seen to be believed. Inside the castle are two Bronze Age barrows, built perhaps 1,500 years before the fortifications. The defenders' water came from a natural spring within the north side. Castle-an-Dinas controlled the main route along mid-

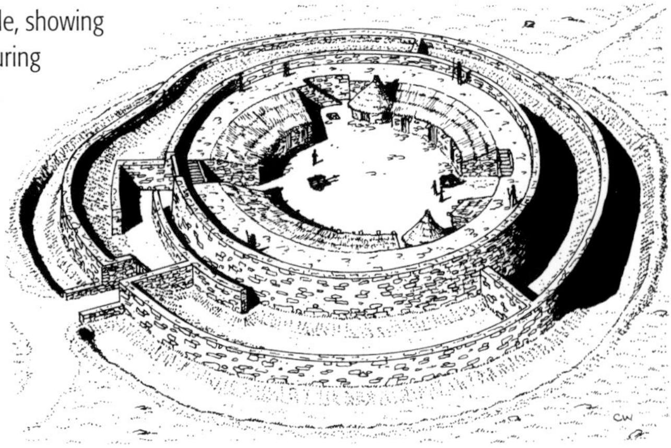

▸ **A drawing of** Chûn Castle, showing how it may have looked during its most recent occupation. Two concentric defensive walls and ditches are visible, together with a staggered protecting entrance. A short distance away from the castle is Chûn Quoit (IMAGE REPRODUCED BY KIND PERMISSION OF CRAIG WEATHERHILL).

Cornwall, and the tin-working area around Roche. Legend tells us Cador, Duke of Cornwall, and King Arthur's mother Ygraine were slain there.

Among other Cornish hillforts are the large double-ringed example at Warbstow Bury, north-west of Launceston; Tregeare Rounds at St Kew; Bury Castle near Cardinham; Castle Pencaire, on Tregonning Hill not far from Breage; Caer Bran at Sancreed; and close to Ludgvan, a second Castle-an-Dinas, a triple stone rampart castle. Near Golant is Castle Dore, guardian of the ancient trade route between Padstow and Fowey but famous more for its reoccupation during the Dark Ages. Could it really have been the site of the legendary tragic triangle between King Mark of Cornwall, his nephew Tristram and his wife Iseult?

Cliff castles were formed from narrow promontories often bounded by steep precipices, barricaded against the mainland using combinations of ditches and embankments. One of the best-preserved cliff castles is at Trevelgue Head near Newquay, which has four close-set ramparts running across a slender neck of land, and a natural chasm over which a drawbridge would have been used. Like others of its type though, Trevelgue wasn't just a castle; evidence survives both of stone houses and fields.

Gurnard's Head, the prominent outcrop near Zennor in West Penwith, bears the remains of a similar triple-rampart stronghold. Other cliff castles can be seen at The Rumps near Polzeath, St Merryn's Winecove Point, Chynalls Point south of Coverack, at Lankidden near St Keverne, and at Rame Head. Treryn Dinas at Treen is defended by five ramparts. An investigation of Kenidjack Castle near St Just in Penwith yielded up thirty pieces of copper and tin near the ramparts, perhaps the local smelter's horde. Indications of permanent habitation are sparse among cliff castles, which were probably used most during turbulent episodes.

▲ **Of Cornwall's cliff** castles Trevelgue is among the best preserved, its ramparts and ditches easy to make out. Today, the narrow chasm separating it from the mainland has been bridged for the benefit of walkers and explorers (Pete London).

▲ **The natural Iron** Age cliff castle of Gurnard's Head in West Penwith, where remains of earthwork defensive ramparts can still be seen (Pete London).

Norman and Medieval Castles

After the Iron Age there was a great lapse of time before further strongholds appeared in Cornwall. But in 1066 William Duke of Normandy defeated Anglo-Saxon Harold II in battle near Hastings, and became King of England. Soon after the Conquest, the Normans began to build great castles as bases for troops to keep the surrounding countryside in order; crushing reminders to local people of who was in charge, who collected their taxes and tithes. During later Norman and medieval times, often the castles were rebuilt or added to; today in Cornwall, ruins of several are still with us.

Under the arriving Normans Cornwall was made an Earldom ruled by Robert of Mortain, King William's half-brother. William gave Robert vast estates across Cornwall, a reward for his loyalty during and after the invasion. To dominate and control the River Tamar's main crossing point at Polson, Robert quickly established a fortress on a high ridge at nearby Dunhevet, which later became known as Launceston. The site was of huge strategic value, overlooking countryside stretching between Bodmin Moor, and Dartmoor in Devon. Robert brought his court to the castle and made it the administrative centre of his territory; gradually a town and market grew around the new construct.

Robert then turned his attention to building a southern fortification. To guard the lower reaches of the River Tamar he picked a site at Trematon above the north bank of the River Lynher, close to present-day Saltash. Trematon Castle was established with wide views across the Hamoaze and Plymouth Sound, on a lofty motte with a bailey extending to the south-west. Cornwall's largest single estate at that time, Trematon was held for Robert by Reginald de Valletort, who also exercised rights over the Tamar; the Valletort family retained Trematon until 1227.

Both Launceston and Trematon castles appear in the 1086 Domesday Book, and both went through several phases of evolution and rebuilding. Launceston and Trematon are motte and bailey castles; other Cornish examples appeared at Cardinham, East Leigh Berrys, Kilkhampton and Tregony. The motte was a hill on which a tower or keep was built, usually a natural geographical feature, but sometimes man-made or an existing rise augmented, the tower containing accommodation for the lord and his retinue. Below was placed the bailey, an enclosed courtyard surrounding the motte, with workshops and stables as well as lodgings for the castle's garrison, huntsmen, cooks, blacksmiths and other craftsmen.

Robert of Mortain's castles were arrangements combining the motte with earthwork revetments and timber walls. But after his son had led an unsuccessful rebellion against King William II, the family's estates including Launceston Castle were confiscated by the Crown. By 1141 the Earldom had passed to Reginald de

Dunstanville, an illegitimate son of King Henry I. We know Reginald began rebuilding Launceston in stone, erecting gatehouses and watch towers, but today very little evidence survives of his labours.

It was another ninety years before Launceston Castle really began to take shape as we know it now. That said, its stone keep, around eighty-five feet in diameter at its widest point – it's slightly ovoid rather than circular – was probably added toward the end of the 1100s. But in 1227 Richard, younger brother of Henry III, became Earl of Cornwall. On top of being wealthy beyond reason, with property right across the southern half of England as well as in Cornwall, Richard was vain and deeply ambitious. He set about Launceston, determined it would be remodelled to show off his great status and position.

By Richard's time there wasn't really much of a military threat around Launceston but nonetheless, inside the keep he added a tall stone tower, while encircling the motte a great ditch was dug. A high stone curtain wall ran round the roughly rectangular bailey, punctuated with defensive towers and replacing the timber walls. Both north and south gatehouses were reconstructed and the accommodation rebuilt in a more opulent way, particularly the great hall where visitors might be entertained. Domestic buildings were much increased, and today evidence remains of the kitchen, pantry, oven and brewing house.

Despite the improvements though, Richard rarely visited Launceston. He spent much of his time in Europe, and with the aid of fat bribes eventually he became King of the Romans. On Richard's death in 1272 his son Edmund inherited the

▲ The earliest surviving image of Launceston Castle, dated 1584, from the hand of cartographer John Norden (AUTHOR'S COLLECTION).

Earldom. But to be nearer the tin trade which provided a hefty proportion of the estate's income, Edmund moved most of his legislative activities south to Lostwithiel. Neglected, Launceston Castle began to fall into disrepair.

In 1337 Edward of Woodstock, the Black Prince, eldest son of Edward III, was created the first Duke of Cornwall; at the time he was only seven years old. The new Duchy comprised the land and property of the old Earldom of Cornwall, together with other estates. But by the time the Duke came of age, Launceston Castle was in a sorry state. Wooden structures had suffered particularly; most of the roofs were rotten, walls ruined, windows out. Pigs had been allowed to rummage around the castle walls and had weakened their foundations.

Repairs were slowly set in hand though the Duke, evidently a thrifty man, ordered they be as economical as possible. Again the great hall was repaired, a good indication of Launceston's real role by then, while the gatehouse was also rebuilt. Over the summer of 1354 the Duke visited his Cornish manors, including his Launceston stronghold. But despite efforts to patch it up, over the following years gradually the underused castle began, once more, to decay. By the end of the fifteenth century only a few public functions were retained there, in particular the shire assizes and an accompanying gaol.

Richard Earl of Cornwall

Richard was the second son of King John, and King Henry III's younger brother. He was born at Winchester during 1209 and when he came of age in 1227 was granted the Earldom of Cornwall. Though he fought in Europe on Henry's behalf, and on three occasions served as Regent, during the early years of his brother's reign frequently their relationship was, to say the least, tense. Richard rebelled against Henry three times and had to be placated with generous gifts. His marriage to Isabel Marshal in 1231 was unpopular with Henry, since his bride's family often opposed the King's policies and wishes.

Richard was defined by fabulous wealth, conceit, and greed for power. He rarely came to Cornwall but nonetheless took great riches from its tin industry, and exerted substantial influence over the shaping of his castles there. The majority of his adult life was spent travelling. He visited the Holy Land, where he successfully negotiated for the release of prisoners, and subsequently spent much time manoeuvring for a European crown of his own. He was offered but rejected the throne of Sicily as too insignificant and far away. Finally, in January 1257 he became King of the Romans, with the help of inducements totalling 28,000 marks to the four German princes who'd voted in support of him.

▲ **A 19thC engraving** of old Launceston town showing the gate in its surrounding wall, the medieval castle exaggeratedly bearing over the town below (AUTHOR'S COLLECTION).

At Trematon too, eventually much had changed. The castle stayed in the de Valletort family until it was acquired from Roger Valletort, the last surviving member, by Richard Earl of Cornwall. Though Richard's main Cornish enthusiasm was the rebuilding of Launceston Castle, he also set in train the construction of a stone keep and curtain wall for Trematon. The new keep, again ovoid, measured around seventy-five feet by sixty feet while the reconstructed bailey was around three hundred feet long.

But it was Richard's son Edmund who finished off Trematon, adding comfortable facilities within the keep for himself and his family. Inside the new curtain wall appeared improved accommodation for his retinue, together with a great hall, a chapel, kitchens and stables. At the end of the century an imposing gatehouse was constructed utilising inner and outer portcullises, its approach covered by two prominent arrow loops. But Edmund died childless in 1300, and Trematon then went through a number of different hands.

In 1307 King Edward II gave the castle to his favourite Piers Gaveston; five years later, after Gaveston's execution it passed to Odo de Ercedekne, whose father was Sheriff of Cornwall. During 1315 the king granted custody of the castle and manor to Thomas of Genely. That year too, Peter Corbet and Henry de Pomeroy claimed possession as descendants of two Valletort heiresses, but unsuccessfully. Around 1328, King Edward III passed Trematon to his brother John of Eltham, who retained it until his death in 1336.

The following year Trematon too passed to the first Duke of Cornwall. Unlike Launceston it had remained in reasonably good order, particularly the lavish gatehouse. It was felt a budget of three pounds a year would be sufficient to maintain the entire castle, which seems rather stingy even by the value of fourteenth-century money. The Black Prince stayed for at least one night there, during 1363, but tales of Trematon being his favourite, oft-visited Cornish castle are folklore.

With the fear of French attack during the 1380s some twenty pounds was spent on repairs by King Richard II, but the invasion never took place. In 1392 the king granted Trematon to John Holland, Earl of Huntingdon. During 1425, King Henry

▲ **Altogether, six motte-**and-bailey castles are known to have been built in Cornwall. Trematon is first recorded in the Domesday Book but over its life was rebuilt and widely modified. This 18thC illustration was included in the works of Cornish antiquary William Borlase (AUTHOR'S COLLECTION).

V gave it to Huntingdon's widow Elizabeth and her second husband Sir John Cornewall; when Sir John died in 1443, Trematon reverted to the Crown. King Edward IV came to the throne during 1461, and later instructed repairs be carried out; parts of the castle became a prison. But after Edward's time Trematon entered a period of neglect. Its most stirring moment was yet to come.

As it survives today Restormel Castle, near Lostwithiel, takes the form of a ringwork, one of six examples built in Cornwall – the others were at Bossiney, Penhallam, Poundstock, Upton and Week St Mary. Restormel's keep sits on a low earth mound, surrounded by a deep, shear-sided man-made ditch, with a substantial bailey area. The origin of the castle can't be dated exactly and it doesn't appear in the Domesday Book. At that time though, a tenant of Robert of Mortain, Norman overlord Turstin the Sheriff, held the Manor of Bodardel which included Restormel; around 1100, his son Baldwin Fitz Turstin constructed a bridge over the nearby River Fowey. It's likely a stronghold appeared then, high on the hill above the valley, as a defensive measure overlooking the new crossing.

Like Launceston and Trematon, the first castle on Restormel's site was an earthwork and timber arrangement; a roughly circular motte with a rectangular bailey containing buildings for artisans, servants and animals. The position dominated the river and, around a mile away, the developing town of Lostwithiel. A growing centre for the export of Cornish tin, for those who controlled it Lostwithiel was a huge financial asset. By the late twelfth century Bodardel had passed to Robert of Cardinham, an influential noble under whose direction the town thrived. Via Robert's son Andrew, then his daughter Isolda, in the summer of 1265 during the Second Barons' War the Manor was temporarily seized by Simon de Montfort, Earl of Leicester. But de Montfort soon fell at the Battle of Evesham bloodbath, while fighting his brother-in-law King Henry III.

Three years later Isolda was swayed, and probably coerced, into parting with Restormel and Lostwithiel once again. Like so much land and property in Cornwall at that time, Bodardel fell under the control of avaricious Richard, Earl of Cornwall. Possession of Isolda's Manor made him even wealthier, and he began the construction of a stone keep for Restormel Castle. When he died Bodardel reverted to the Crown for a short time, before passing to his son Edmund.

Not least for economic reasons, Edmund decided to concentrate his seat of power in the area. As well as moving most of Cornwall's civic functions south from Launceston, at Lostwithiel he commissioned a striking building containing the Shire Hall, the Hall of Exchequer, and the Coinage Hall, where tin was assayed and duty paid. Later the site became known as the Duchy Palace. It's probable Edmund also gave the final shape to Restormel Castle.

▲ **Before it was** reclaimed by the then Ministry of Works, Restormel Castle had been lost under a leafy shroud. When the encroaching trees, bushes and moss were cut away the castle was found surprisingly intact, its interior rooms well-preserved (AUTHOR'S COLLECTION).

Restormel's circular shell keep is just under 130 feet in diameter and made of local shillet, flat-layered stone. The keep enclosed comfortable first-floor chambers which faced into the central courtyard, for Edmund, his family and his immediate entourage. It also housed a great hall with an adjoining kitchen, together with a well, lavatories and a guardroom. Several cellars, actually positioned at ground-level, were built under the accommodation. A chapel protruded through the keep on its north-east side, while the entrance opposite was protected by a prominent gatehouse. Like numbers of castles at the time, externally Restormel's keep was plastered then lime-washed to give it a vivid white finish, which must have helped send a powerful statement across the surrounding countryside. Restormel's bailey, its perimeter gradually rebuilt in stone, continued to provide timber quarters for workers and animals.

Really, Edmund's castle hovered between fortress and status symbol. It was strategically-placed of course, and incorporated military features; a crenellated parapet, a water-filled moat, a drawbridge and above the entrance, arrow-slits. Yet

The Duchy of Cornwall

The Duchy of Cornwall was created in March 1337 from the former Earldom of Cornwall, by King Edward III for his son and heir Prince Edward – later known as the Black Prince. As Duke of Cornwall, Edward acquired Launceston, Restormel, Tintagel and Trematon Castles. Not all of Cornwall was included in the Duchy, while its other possessions were spread across Devon, Herefordshire and Somerset. The Duchy's principal purpose has always been to provide an income from its assets for the first-born son of the English monarch, through management of its lands and properties.

In Edward's day and afterwards, a particularly lucrative source of revenue from the Duchy was the Cornish tin industry. After Henry VIII died, during the reign of childless Elizabeth I there was no Duke. To date there have been twenty-four Dukes of Cornwall, thirteen of whom have become monarchs. Since 1993 the Duke's income from the Duchy has been voluntarily subject to income tax.

several of Restormel's main rooms featured large windows, prestigious at that time, set in the shell; a deer park took shape in the surrounding grounds, at one time Cornwall's largest. But when Edmund died, again the Manor reverted to the Crown and care by a succession of managers.

The Black Prince visited Restormel twice; preceding each call the castle was duly spruced up, its accommodation renovated, splendid stores laid in. During August 1354 the Prince arrived on horseback with his retinue; eight years later, at Christmas he called again, during a break from his overseas military campaigns. The Prince stayed at Restormel until the following spring, all the while organising a trip to France for he'd recently been created Prince of Aquitaine by his father. Sailing from Plymouth, the Prince never returned to Cornwall and like Launceston Castle, after his death in 1376 Restormel began a slow but steady decline. Subsequent Dukes of Cornwall paid little interest in the castle except for occasional, half-hearted attempts to patch it up.

Set on a dramatic north coast peninsula, linked to the mainland by the remains of a narrow isthmus, Tintagel Castle is awash with myth and fable: King Arthur, Merlin the Magician, the Knights of the Round Table. And fable it is. Even if he really existed, there's no hard evidence to associate Arthur with the castle, despite what today's tourist industry may suggest.

Over the fourth and fifth centuries it's possible the site of Tintagel was occupied or at least visited by Romano British people, though the evidence is slim. Tintagel was also where the Dark Age Celtic kings of Dumnonia are said to have held court. This has more substance; remains excavated from the site indicate it was populated between around 400 and 600 AD. The relics found include items which at the time would have been considered lavish; decorated pottery and glassware from the Mediterranean. In several places too, low walls, foundations and signs of huts are thought to originate from that time. The inference is of occupation by wealthy traders, possibly even Cornwall's Dark Age rulers.

It was chronicler Geoffrey of Monmouth who first linked Arthur and Tintagel, in his work History of the Kings in Britain written in around 1136. But Geoffrey was a storyteller, his accounts more tales than historical studies. He brought Arthur forward from a small-time sixth-century king to a conqueror, and relocated him from a modest realm nearer to Wales than Cornwall.

Around 1233 Richard Earl of Cornwall acquired the site, and three years later began building a substantial castle. There was no strategic reason for the location of the new stronghold, and Earl Richard rarely stayed there, but most of today's ruins are his work. Perhaps his intention was to impress the Cornish with a truly profligate display of wealth and power. Richard placed the entrance to his castle on the

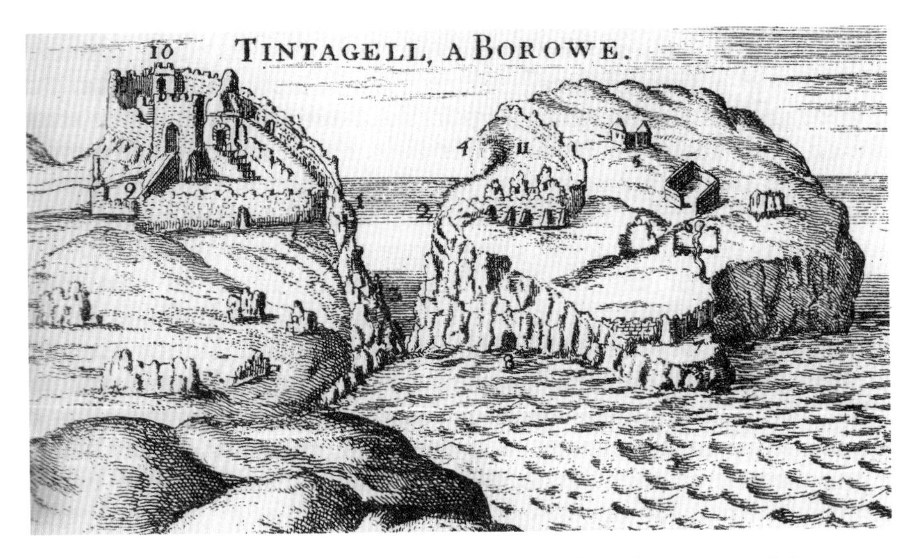

▲ **Tintagel Castle depicted** by John Norden during the late sixteenth century. The isthmus linking the promontory has partially fallen away and most of the buildings seem in poor shape, but the landside baileys are shown as reasonably intact (AUTHOR'S COLLECTION).

▲ Tintagel Castle photographed from the air during the 1950s. Outlines of the two impressively-sized mainland courtyards are to the left. On the promontory, ruins survive of the courtyard and the hall; to the right, the chapel (AUTHOR'S COLLECTION).

mainland; two huge baileys were built, surrounded by high curtain walls, with a gate tower guarding the access. As with other baileys at the time, those at Tintagel would have provided for labourers and soldiers, workshops and stables. On the peninsula a great hall was built, within a courtyard surrounded by a curtain wall which ran to the cliff edge. The hall was the castle's main building, where guests could be entertained, with accommodation for Richard and his retinue as well as a kitchen and store.

On Richard's death Tintagel passed to his son. But Edmund was more interested in moving south to Restormel, and the castle became neglected; when he died during 1300 it reverted to the Crown. The first Duke of Cornwall acquired Tintagel in 1337 by when it was in marked decline, many its buildings collapsed, not least the great hall which had partly fallen into the sea following a landslip. The Black Prince made good some of the damage; the hall was rebuilt, though it was of more modest proportions than its predecessor, while the stables were refurbished.

During the 1380s, fearing an attack by the French, King Richard II set repairs in motion to Tintagel's curtain wall. Richard also used Tintagel as a prison. Among those locked up were John de Northampton, Lord Mayor of London between 1381 and 1382, accused of treason by his rival (and successor) Sir Nicholas Brembre.

Tintagel passed from custodian to custodian but little was done to improve its condition. Although minor repairs were carried out during the reign of King Henry VII, by the mid-sixteenth century the castle was deserted. A great chunk of the isthmus between mainland and peninsula had given way, taking the gate and drawbridge with it.

Deep in the Cornish west near Penzance stands a further stronghold stemming from the Middle Ages: the priory of St Michael's Mount. At first sight, especially today, the Mount doesn't seem a practical military castle, a purpose-built defensive fortification. But its very location atop the craggy island dominates the eastern side of Mount's Bay and lends it an obvious strategic credibility. Historically the Mount helped secure the harbour; it never acquired the architecture of a typical castle, but at times it did play a noteworthy military role in Cornish affairs.

The priory was founded in 1135 by Bernard Le Bec, who was also Abbot of Mont St Michel, the French place of pilgrimage at the mouth of the Couesnon River in Normandy. The Cornish cell was very much a possession of its parent, the monks there having allegiance to their French seniors, which in times of war caused suspicion of disloyalty and confiscation of wealth. Today, the medieval buildings that survive at St Michael's Mount are mostly part of the priory, protected by fortifications which include two towers, along with the west range and parts of the curtain wall.

In 1193, with King Richard I held for ransom overseas, the Mount was seized by Henry de Pomeroy, a supporter of the monarch's treacherous brother John Lackland. To gain entry de Pomeroy disguised his men as pilgrims, but on Richard's release the Priory was soon given up; Henry died by his own hand.

Until the fifteenth century the Mount retained its links with France, but during 1423 finally passed to the control of Sion Abbey at Twickenham. Two years later the causeway connecting the island to the mainland was built, and the Mount led a reasonably peaceful life until the Wars of the Roses. In the autumn of 1473 the Lancastrian Earl of Oxford landed from France, entering the Mount by the same subterfuge as de Pomeroy. He and his men withstood a four-month siege by the Sheriff of Cornwall Sir Henry Bodrugan, and Sir John Arundell of Lanherne; Bodrugan was discharged for letting food into the Mount and replaced by Richard Fortescue, while Arundell was killed in a skirmish. After a relentless blockade by

Fortescue, combined with promises of pardons, finally in February 1474 the Earl and his depleted force were forced to surrender; Oxford was exiled.

During September 1497 the Mount witnessed another would-be invader; pretender Perkin Warbeck's ill-starred attempt to dethrone Henry VII. Warbeck's wife Lady Catherine Gordon stayed at the Mount while her husband's forces marched on Exeter, but the rebels were heavily defeated. Eventually Warbeck was hanged; by contrast his widow joined Henry's court. The Mount settled back to its ordered life, but Henry's third child would cause profound changes.

▲ **John Norden's late** sixteenth-century illustration of St Michael's Mount is fanciful in terms of the site's towering height and conical shape, but does show the crenellated defensive works of the priory (AUTHOR'S COLLECTION).

Tudor Castles

The Cornish castles built before Tudor times were used to control their neighbouring areas. But by the late medieval age, dangers to Britain's security had begun to emerge from abroad, threats which were sustained through the Tudor period. As maritime commerce grew too, the positions of Cornwall and the Isles of Scilly in guarding the western approaches and the English Channel increased in strategic importance. New Cornish fortifications appeared during the reigns of King Henry VIII and Queen Elizabeth I, to help defend the country from its overseas enemies.

As a response to threats particularly from France and Spain, Henry built a string of coastal artillery castles from the Isles of Scilly to easternmost Cornwall at Mount Edgecombe, and beyond. By the Tudor age cannons were at the forefront of modern warfare, able to fire ball or shot at enemy ships hundreds of yards away and ideal for safeguarding the British coastline. But since the ships could fire back, Henry's Cornish castles sat lower to the ground, sited in less exposed positions than their forebears.

At the mouth of the River Fowey St Catherine's Castle was constructed, but the entrance to Falmouth's vast deep-water harbour became the home of two much larger fortifications: squat cousins Pendennis Castle on the western side, and

Henry VIII's enemies

What caused Henry VIII to build his string of castles along the south coast? During 1533, arising from his divorce of Catherine of Aragon and marriage to Anne Boleyn, Pope Clement VII had excommunicated him. The following year Henry proclaimed himself head of the Protestant Church of England. His subsequent dissolution of the monasteries considerably increased his wealth, but Henry's relations with Catholic France and Spain, never sparkling, deteriorated sharply.

In fact by the 1530s Henry had twice invaded France, though without sustained success. Enmity remained between the two nations, while Catherine's nephew was Charles V, ruler of Spain. In 1538, France and Spain became allies, while at the end of the year Pope Paul III excommunicated him for a second time. By then Henry was expanding his navy – he became known as the 'Father of the English Navy' – but the threat of invasion was so great that during the late 1530s and early 1540s he instigated a hurried assessment of likely sites all along the Channel coast at which to build defences. Pendennis and St Mawes were completed by 1545.

▲ **Looking out to** sea at the mouth of Falmouth harbour, Little Dennis, the first element of Pendennis Castle to be constructed (PETE LONDON).

St Mawes a mile and a half across the bay to the east. During the early 1550s a stronghold appeared on the Isles of Scilly, to protect Tresco's New Grimsby harbour.

Initially, the Pendennis and St Mawes sites received just a single tower each, housing small cannon. Little Dennis was built in around 1539, while across the water to the east a matching example appeared. But during the early 1540s Pendennis Castle itself was built, on a site leased from the prominent Killigrew gentry of nearby Arwenack. Design of Pendennis was probably influenced by the Moravian military architect Stephan von Haschenperg; today its builder is lost to us, but may have been John Killigrew. Granite for the castle was quarried from nearby Mabe.

The core of Pendennis took the form of a large central tower, circular in section and around thirty-five feet tall, with walls some eleven feet thick. In the tower's basement were the kitchen and store room; immediately above were quarters for the garrison, together with positions for seven cannon arranged with an impressively broad field of fire. The top room was equipped with seven more cannon, and on the tower roof was room for a third group of seven. At the top of the tower too was placed a small observation turret, vital to keep a careful lookout, its view around two hundred feet above sea level.

◄ **Pendennis Castle:** a 1734 engraving by Samuel and Nathaniel Buck. Henry VIII's fortification is somewhat out of scale with its miniature surroundings (AUTHOR'S COLLECTION).

Early in the life of Pendennis it was decided to dispense with the lower-level cannon within the tower and move them outside, which allowed improved accommodation for the garrison, and so the exterior gun platform surrounding the tower was developed. The platform was built using sixteen flat sides, and was arranged to accommodate fourteen cannon. Around its perimeter a deep defensive dry moat was dug.

The entrance to Pendennis was covered by a square building of two storeys, added after the tower. Here the castle captain lived, in comfortable accommodation; sleeping quarters, a living room, his own kitchen. A drawbridge crossed the moat and beyond was a guardhouse.

Across the Carrick Roads, St Mawes was constructed at the tip of a small isthmus by the Porthcuil River, overlooking the main deep-water channel into Falmouth harbour. Smaller than Pendennis, its guns covered the harbour mouth in conjunction with those of its cousin. Oddly though, the castle was built near higher ground on its eastern side, a vulnerable position if foreign troops were to land. The building programme was overseen by Sir Thomas Treffry of the renowned Cornish family, and the bill for the new castle came to around £5,000.

St Mawes' keep was a three-storey circular arrangement, atop of which was placed a small watch-tower. To the keep were attached three semi-circular artillery bastions, one to each side and one forward, in a trilobe planform. Bastions were platforms designed to house artillery, with a much lower profile than the walls of medieval castles. By Tudor times, development of increasingly destructive cannon meant attacking forces could more easily damage or breach the high, conspicuous walls of older castles, but the new type of fortification presented a somewhat smaller target. St Mawes' bastions were positioned to allow their guns to deliver dense, overlapping fields of fire across one another. The castle was surrounded by a deep ditch cut out from the rock, again with a fixed stone bridge connecting a separate guard-house.

In the keep were billeted both officers and men, the officers on the second floor and the men below. At the lowest level were the kitchen and stores. The garrison seems to have varied between fewer than twenty men and up to a hundred, numbers naturally rising at times of threat.

Above the accommodation was a gun platform with provision for eight cannon with an all-round field of fire. Each of the bastions was arranged on two levels. The central bastion housed five cannon on its lower, enclosed platform, with four more in the open air above. The east and west bastions were constructed with three main cannon ports at the lower level, and positions for five more cannon above. Understandably, the magazine containing gunpowder for the cannon was placed well away from the castle, while at the shoreline a blockhouse was built, holding three more guns.

By the time St Mawes was finished over thirty assorted cannon had been installed, but as well as up-to-the-minute technology the castle armoury included old-fashioned bows and arrows for closer combat against individuals, together with muskets. And though it was a small castle at around a hundred feet across its outer

▲ St Mawes Castle seen from roughly west, captured in an engraving by M J Starling from a drawing by Thomas Allom, 1831 (AUTHOR'S COLLECTION).

▲ **St Mawes from** the water; for sightseers a ferry connects the castle with Falmouth. The forward and eastern bastions are in view, dominated by the central tower and above, the look-out position (PETE LONDON).

batteries and some sixty-five feet in height, St Mawes was certainly well-adorned. Great depictions of shields were embedded in its outer walls, together with Latin inscriptions praising King Henry, organised by Treffry who wanted command of the castle. When building was completed at the end of 1547 he was duly made St Mawes' first captain, but following his departure it was the Cornish Vyvyan family who provided governors until well into the seventeenth century.

To the east, Fowey's St Catherine's Castle had been completed during 1540. St Catherine's provided artillery defence of the town's harbour, and like St Mawes was masterminded by Sir Thomas Treffry. Around 150 feet up on the rugged clifftop of St Catherine's Head, on the western bank of the estuary, it was smaller than its Falmouth cousins and replaced two earlier fortifications. St Catherine's was based round a two-storey D-shaped blockhouse with splayed gun ports and high battlements, the curved portion of which pointed out to sea to maximise the field of fire. Typically the castle held six cannon situated in the lower level, while officers and men were accommodated above.

By the mid-sixteenth century St Michael's Mount was no longer a place of pilgrimage. Henry VIII had seized its wealth, and because of its obvious strategic position its main purpose became military. Henry died in 1547, and was succeeded by nine-year old King Edward VI. A Council of Regency was established to control the country, headed by the king's ambitious uncle the Earl of Hertford, who became Duke of Somerset and Lord Protector. Somerset was an ardent Protestant; under a new Act of Uniformity the use of English, rather than Latin, in church services was enforced across the country through the introduction of the Book of Common Prayer. In Cornwall, an area of wide Roman Catholic loyalty with its own language outside worship, this caused fear and deep resentment.

For the Cornish people, the change was the final outrage in a succession of anti-Catholic actions inflicted by a distant, foreign government. Removal of Catholic symbols from places of worship; dissolution of Penryn's Glasney College in 1548 and the attendant diminution of Cornish identity; the Launceston Castle massacre by the authorities of twenty-eight Cornishmen following the murder in Helston of a Protestant enforcer. Finally, the following summer, aggravated by spiralling food prices, bitterness boiled into armed revolt. The rebels' leader was the Governor of

▲ **At the mouth** of the Fowey River, bijou St Catherine's Castle depicted in an engraving dated 1786 (AUTHOR'S COLLECTION).

St Michael's Mount and commander of its garrison, devout Catholic Sir Humphrey Arundell of Helland.

During the campaign, once Arundell had left his base some members of the Cornish gentry, including Sir William Godolphin, sought refuge in the Mount; they were promptly besieged by Arundell's troops. The attackers built great trusses of hay below the buildings, to which they set fire; the resulting smoke-screen obscured their subsequent assault. It seems there was little resistance and surrender of the Mount swiftly followed. Godolphin was imprisoned in the gaol at Launceston Castle, held by the rebels at that time.

Trematon, though it had seen much better days, had been leased to Sir Richard Grenville, a supporter of the king. The castle was surrounded by Arundell's men, led by Robert Smyth of St Germans. Since the rebels had no siege equipment Grenville remained safe inside but even so, by night many of his men dropped from the castle walls and disappeared. Grenville chose to parley with the rebels, meeting them at a sally-gate in the castle wall. But the rebels ignored the conventions of war and simply pushed past the elderly Grenville; they fell on the troops remaining inside Trematon, who swiftly surrendered. The prisoners were treated with grim cruelty, while Grenville joined Sir William Godolphin at Launceston.

The Prayer Book Rebellion

During the summer of 1549, Catholic Cornwall rose against the imposition of the English Book of Common Prayer under Edward VI's Reformation. A Cornish army gathered, forming two groups which advanced eastward; the principal took Plymouth and besieged Exeter. Eight demands were sent to the London government; the last stated "and so we the Cornyshe men utterly refuse thys newe English". Driven before them, the English sought help in the shape of Lord John Russell, who sent for reinforcements including Italian and German mercenary troops.

While Exeter remained besieged, several bloody encounters took place and at first the rebels more than held their own. But the battle of Clyst St Mary on 5 August left hundreds of Cornish dead or taken captive; Russell had the prisoners, all nine hundred of them, murdered. Exeter was relieved and though the Cornish force regrouped, at the Battle of Sampford Courtenay on 17 August, greatly outnumbered, they were decisively defeated. During the retreat that followed, many of the remaining Cornish troops were killed by Russell's men. Subsequently the rebels' ringleaders were caught and executed, while hundreds of ordinary Cornish people were abused or murdered during barbaric English reprisals.

▲ **The oldest part** of St Michael's Mount, the priory, seen from the east. Its stained-glass windows, and the artefacts inside are truly beautiful (PETE LONDON).

◀ Engraving of Trematon Castle by J C Sparrow, published by P Hooper during 1787. Its curtain wall has tumbled down in places, and the keep is damaged (AUTHOR'S COLLECTION).

▼ Pendennis Castle seen from the west. To the left, the bridge over the dry moat and accommodation for the castle's captain, with the main tower and circular bastion to the right. Overseeing all, the look-out tower is perched above (PETE LONDON).

The so-called Prayer Book Rebellion was marked by brutal battles between Cornish forces and the King's troops supported by foreign mercenaries. Defeat of the rebels was closely followed by the victors' unbridled, sadistic retribution. Arundell and his confederates were executed and it's estimated that in all, over five thousand Cornish people died during the campaign and its aftermath.

During the latter years of the sixteenth century antagonism between Britain and Spain over political and religious differences continued, and clashes increased between their fleets. In 1585, with Elizabeth I on the throne, the two nations went to war. Cornwall's coastal castles waited, their garrisons reinforced. Three years later, after intermittent naval engagements finally the enemy moved. A huge Spanish

invasion fleet, the great Armada, arrived off Cornwall; at St Michael's Mount, on the priory tower a beacon was lit to warn of the approaching force. But the Spanish sailed east past the waiting defenders, and eventually were devastated by a combination of the English fleet and bad weather.

During 1595 the governor of St Mawes, Hannibal Vyvyan, sent word to Sir Francis Drake at Plymouth that four Spanish galleys had raided Mousehole, Newlyn, Paul, and Penzance, and requested ships be released from Devon to repel the invaders. That time though, having caused widespread damage, the enemy melted away. But during the following year the Spanish assembled a second armada, their intention to take Falmouth harbour as a beachhead to launch a full-scale military campaign. Fortunately, like the earlier attempt, Spain's fleet was beaten back from Britain by the elements.

Nonetheless, at that time some five hundred levied men joined the regular soldiers at Pendennis. By the end of the century the castle's fortifications had been greatly reinforced under a programme masterminded by Sir Walter Raleigh, professional soldier Sir Nicholas Parker and Paul Ive, an experienced designer of military defences. A huge outer defensive ring was built, from which sharply-angled bastions protruded. Henry VIII's castle sat within the south-eastern end of the new defences. Pendennis's fresh bastions were designed to house demicannons and culverins for long-range attacks, together with smaller muzzle-loading handguns for closer targets, all given wide fields of fire across the mouth of the harbour and out to sea.

But just after Ive's work was completed, in 1603 King James I came to the throne; relations with Spain and France improved. Cornwall's castles became less important, their garrisons were reduced and expenditure cut. St Mawes' strength was sharply diminished while Pendennis's garrison, unpaid, were reduced to eating limpets to supplement their meagre rations.

By the end of the sixteenth century too, generally the Duchy's old medieval castles were in poor shape. Trematon was derelict, its use by Sir Francis Drake as a temporary treasure store long over. All that remained were its shell keep, a good portion of the curtain wall, a building for the keeper and a small gaol. Tintagel had been deserted throughout almost the entire century and had finally crumbled to ruins, its few surviving buildings in a dangerous state.

By contrast though, a drawing of Launceston Castle made at that time by itinerant cartographer John Norden shows it in reasonably good repair. In places we can see the outer wall is crumbling, but within the bailey the buildings appear in fair order. Launceston's gaol continued in service, and the site was also used to stage the amusement (for the audience) of public hangings. But abandoned Restormel was in such a sorry state that Norden regretfully concluded it should be demolished, its stonework reused; fortunately his suggestion wasn't taken up.

The Isles of Scilly

Just twenty-eight miles off the southwest tip of Cornwall lie the Isles of Scilly, an archipelago of six inhabited islands and a shoal of small rocky islets. The islands provide Britain's most westerly anchorages; by medieval times, as nautical traffic grew, their isolated communities faced potential foes particularly from France and Spain.

A first attempt at providing land-based protection for the islanders was made during the mid-thirteenth century when Ennor castle appeared on St Mary's, principal of the islands. The castle was built on a small granite outcrop near the present-day Old Town Bay. A small shell keep castle, Ennor's walled courtyard covered an area of around seventy-five feet by fifty-five feet, and its earliest surviving reference is in a deed of 1244.

By 1306, with King Edward I on the throne, Ennor was in the hands of Sir Ranulph de Blanchminster who was appointed its constable. Ranulph paid the king a yearly rent; either 6s 8d (34p), or three hundred puffins. During medieval times the birds, native to the Islands, were valuable; they were classed as fish and so could be eaten during Lent. Ranulph was responsible for finding just twelve men-at-arms to populate the new fortress but he seems to have failed in that duty; he also imprisoned the King's coroner during a visit to the islands to hold an assize.

In 1337 Ennor was included among the assets of the new Duchy of Cornwall, along with the rest of Scilly. A garrison was maintained intermittently, not least at

▲ Elizabeth 1's Star Castle looms over the waters it dominates around the western peninsula of St Mary's (AUTHOR'S COLLECTION).

some of the tense times two centuries later, during Henry VIII's reign. By 1554 the castle was in use as an armoury, equipped with five cannons for the protection of Old Town harbour; at that time the garrison is said to have numbered 150 men. But during the reign of Elizabeth I, Ennor entered a decline and eventually was partly dismantled.

During the early 1550s with Edward VI as king, and against a background, once again, of souring relations with the French, work began on a castle for the island of Tresco. The new stronghold was built by Sir Thomas Godolphin, intended to protect the northern entrance of Tresco's substantial New Grimsby anchorage. Cannon were positioned in two tiers inside a protruding five-sided gun platform, overlooking the water to the castle's western side. Behind the guns were domestic quarters: a guardroom, hall, kitchen, and billets. The castle was modest, its overall footprint around twenty yards square.

But the location chosen was poor. The castle was positioned at the western side and highest point of what became known as Castle Down, but its elevation markedly restricted its cannons' ability to train on the water below, and so prevent shipping entering the harbour. If the cannon were depressed too far, the ball would simply roll out of the barrel and down the hill. On top of that rather elementary weakness,

▲ Star Castle, seen during the late nineteenth century. Today the castle is a hotel, its sea views spectacular (AUTHOR'S COLLECTION).

no real thought had been given to defence of the castle in the event of assault from its land side. It became clear Godolphin's creation was something of a folly, and if New Grimsby were to be properly protected a new castle would have to be built.

By the end of the sixteenth century, on St Mary's the Isles' stoutest and most impressive castle was complete. Following the destruction of Spain's armada Elizabeth I commanded the islands' governor Sir Francis Godolphin, Thomas's son, to build a substantial artillery castle on St Mary's. England and Spain were still at war; the fortification would prevent a regrouped Spanish force seizing a westernmost base, and would also protect the islands from pirates.

Perhaps mindful of his father's gaffe, Francis engaged the experienced coastal defence engineer Robert Adams to build the castle. Work started during mid-1593, the site a peninsula named The Hugh at the western side of the island, overlooking the harbour entrance. Adams saw to it that by the end of the following year the castle was complete, a rapid and efficient programme. It's probable that stonework from discarded Ennor Castle was taken to help with the new project. Adams completed his work despite the parsimony of Elizabeth's government, which paid the construction bills late and then only partially; Godolphin funded the balance of £600 and finally, in mid-1603 it was King James I who settled up for the Crown.

Initially the Islands' new fortification was named Stella Mariae, but this was soon altered to Star Castle. The stronghold was the product of an imaginative mind well in touch with current developments in defensive works. Surrounded by a deep dry moat, the ramparts took the planform of an eight-pointed star, from which the castle derived its name. Each of the points allowed for angled, dense fields of fire from cannon and musketry though a series of loops positioned on the ramparts' skirting walls, across the open ground beyond the castle. Three sally-ports were built into the walls, while the castle's entrance was guarded by a portcullis and a cannon; over the entrance was carved the inscription 'ER 1593' and adjacent was placed a modest bell-tower.

Inside the walls was a two-storey central block with accommodation for the summertime garrison strength of a lieutenant, three gunners and twenty-six soldiers, together with a kitchen and a basement storage area. After the main building programme had been completed a wall was built across the neck of the peninsula. But enemies didn't come; though from time to time it received prisoners and exiles, for over forty years Star Castle sat peacefully on its beautiful island.

Civil War

When Britain erupted into civil war during 1642, in the main Cornwall supported the Royalist cause. By the following year, following a brief but violent struggle in the north, the Duchy was secured for King Charles I. Two of Cornwall's medieval castles became garrisoned by Royalist forces, the importance of their strategic locations eclipsing their decay as fortifications. The Tudor castles at Pendennis and St Mawes also received troops, together with those on the Isles of Scilly, though they'd been built to repel offshore invaders rather than those from beyond the Tamar.

At the outbreak of war Launceston Castle was held by Sir Richard Buller for Parliament. At the appearance of a substantial Royalist force under Sir Ralph Hopton though, Buller took flight. Hopton occupied the site, patching the castle up and in the following year defeating an attempt to besiege him. During 1644 though, Launceston was briefly occupied by Parliamentarian Robert Devereux, 3rd Earl of Essex. But with Essex's comprehensive defeat at Lostwithiel in September, Launceston again reverted to the Royalists.

At Restormel too, at first Parliamentary soldiers occupied the crumbling castle and an attempt was made to renovate it. Under Essex's instruction, the main window of the chapel was blocked up and a platform erected for a cannon sited across the valley to the east. But in August 1644 Restormel was besieged by a Royalist force under Sir Richard Grenville, whose forebear had occupied Trematon during the war

The Civil War

King Charles I alienated many of his subjects through his religious beliefs, and his resolve to govern without Parliament. As religious and political views polarised, in 1642 civil war broke out. By the following year, Charles' forces looked well-placed to win, but Parliament formed an alliance with Scotland. At the battle of Marston Moor in 1644 the Scots helped defeat Charles' army, while at Naseby the following year his forces were decimated by Parliament, and the Royalists were lost.

Charles surrendered to the Scottish forces rather than to Parliament, but the Scots handed him over. Even while captive, Charles refused to alter his views on religion and government, and in 1649 his supporters began a second conflict. Opinion grew among Parliament that while he remained alive the country could never be at peace. Charles was accused of high treason, tried, found guilty, and in January 1649, beheaded. In place of the monarchy a republic was established named the Commonwealth, headed by Charles' Parliamentarian adversary Oliver Cromwell.

▲ **A rather romanticised**, larger-than-life Restormel, seen overgrown through the eyes of Thomas Allom, and engraved by W LePetit. The illustration was published in the journal Devon & Cornwall Illustrated during 1832 (AUTHOR'S COLLECTION).

of 1549. After a few days, pounded by artillery, the castle fell, but the victors had merely wished to dislodge their enemy. Restormel was left unoccupied and was never again inhabited.

Trematon Castle had deteriorated so much that neither side felt it worth seizing; only the gaoler and his charges remained there, occupying two of the few intact rooms. Tintagel's ruins too were ignored. To the west though, St Michael's Mount became a Royalist base under Sir Francis Bassett, who'd bought it in 1640. The Mount, overlooking its prized anchorage, was reinforced using Bassett's own money, and a garrison raised of fifty men. New gun platforms appeared and initially, fourteen new cannon; eventually thirty arrived. In 1645 new redoubts were constructed on the quay of the harbour, together with a smaller defensive position to guard the well. During that year Francis died; his brother Sir Arthur succeeded him.

As the war dragged on, gradually Parliament gained ascendancy over the King. In June 1645, at the battle of Naseby in Northamptonshire, Charles's principal army was crushed by the New Model Army under Parliament's commander-in-chief, Sir Thomas Fairfax. From then, the Royalist cause was in effect broken. Bristol fell during September 1645, as the Parliamentarians advanced westward.

▲ **Launceston Castle today**; its steeply rising motte and tall inner tower provide a vertigo-inducing experience for the visitor, but the views take some beating (PETE LONDON).

That month, Launceston Castle was visited by the Prince of Wales, the future King Charles II, following his withdrawal from Exeter. Later in the year Sir Richard Grenville began yet another attempt to renovate Launceston's fortifications. But during the early part of 1646 the King's forces in Cornwall began to come apart. On 18 January, Grenville resigned his commission after refusing to serve under Hopton. He was arrested at Launceston for insubordination and via the gaol within the castle he'd helped secure, was imprisoned at St Michael's Mount.

Fairfax entered Launceston on 25 February; Hopton fell back on Falmouth. It became plain the Prince of Wales would have to leave Cornwall, quickly, and he too travelled to Falmouth; after a brief stay at Pendennis Castle he made ship bound for the Isles of Scilly. On 14 March Hopton surrendered to Fairfax at Tresillian Bridge, just east of Truro; he agreed to disband the Royalist western army.

Hopton had sent two hundred soldiers to defend St Michael's Mount, but by the early spring half of them had deserted. The Prince of Wales stayed there briefly during his passage west; shortly after he'd left, a Parliamentary force arrived commanded by a Colonel Hammond. To avoid a long siege and mindful of the wider picture of defeat, on 23 April Sir Arthur Bassett surrendered. Terms were generous, the victors equally relieved a protracted blockade wouldn't be called for. Bassett left, banished to St Mary's, and Colonel John St Aubyn was appointed Governor of the Mount.

At the outbreak of war Pendennis Castle was still in a state of decay, undermanned and under-gunned, but despite its meagre resources retained advantages of position and physical strength. From July 1643 its Royalist occupiers were commanded by the elderly Colonel John Arundell of Trerice. For most of the war Pendennis remained calm but as Parliamentarian forces approached from the east, action grew closer.

After Hopton's surrender, during mid-March Fairfax demanded John Arundell lay down his arms. But by then around a thousand troops were garrisoned in Pendennis, and Arundell refused to yield. A siege followed, marked by mutual bombardment, and though the defenders grew terribly short of provisions their resistance continued. Not only was Pendennis besieged from the land; off Falmouth lay the ships of Captain Batten, scouring the seas for Royalist supply vessels bringing food and ammunition. Desertions increased, powder and shot became low.

Finally, his garrison starving, Arundell was forced to surrender. On 17 August the men marched out led by their brave commander, heads high and drums beating, allowed by the Parliamentarians to keep their arms and colours. Such was the deprivation they'd experienced that shortly afterwards, some died.

St Mawes Castle hadn't proved as resilient. Like Pendennis it had suffered from neglect over previous years, particularly after around 1603 when Sir Francis Vyvyan became Captain. It seems Vyvyan ran St Mawes into the ground financially. From time to time he received monies for the castle's upkeep; whether the funds were spent properly is doubtful. In 1632 Vyvyan was tried and cashiered by the Court of Star Chamber, a central supervisory judicial body, for 'practising a variety of deceptions'.

▲ **Today the interior** of Pendennis Castle has been sympathetically refurbished, with displays and information boards adding to the visitor's enjoyment. Here, inside the central tower, a cannon is deployed (Pete London).

In around 1636 Major Hannibal Bonython was appointed Captain, determined to improve the fortunes of St Mawes. Funding was vital and without agreement, Bonython began collecting substantial harbour dues from ships visiting Falmouth, previously the sole preserve of Pendennis. This self-help led to advanced animosity with Sir William Killigrew, then Governor of the western castle; Bonython continued unabashed. But though he raised money and harangued the government, supplies and arms were slow in coming through.

And once war had broken out, all Bonython's labours proved pointless. St Mawes had been built to oppose attack from the seas; from landward it was an easy target, positioned dangerously near higher ground on its eastern side. In March 1646 Fairfax and his Parliamentary forces arrived and surrounded the castle. Without a fight, Bonython capitulated.

The fall of Pendennis marked the end of the Civil War in Cornwall, but the Isles of Scilly had also formed a Royalist stronghold. Tresco's oddly-sited castle received a substantial bastioned earthwork, together with an outer ditch, built to its eastward side in an attempt to make it less vulnerable to attack from the land. During the spring of 1646 the Prince of Wales stayed at Star Castle on St Mary's, before sailing to the Royalist enclave of Jersey. Those were the high spots of the islands' Civil War, and in the following September they surrendered to Fairfax's Parliamentarian forces. To govern the islands, Fairfax appointed a Colonel Buller.

But after a year of uneasy armistice and political chaos across Britain, during the spring of 1648 numerous pro-Royalist uprisings broke out. In northern and southern England, and in Wales, the second Civil War began. The Isles of Scilly too rose against the Parliamentarians; while Colonel Buller attended church, his garrison mutinied. The broader Royalist rebellion was put down by early 1649, King Charles I executed at the end of January, but the Isles continued their allegiance to his son Charles, Prince of Wales. In February Sir John Grenville arrived, appointed Governor by the Prince. That month too, the Scottish Parliament declared Charles lawful heir to the thrones of Britain, France and Ireland.

▲ A the western end of its perimeter St Mawes incorporates a five-cannon saluting battery positioned on a levelled platform (PETE LONDON).

Grenville added defensive earthwork banks around Star Castle and the Hugh, together with more cannon. From his domain the new Governor encouraged privateering, though almost certainly without letters of marque for his ships; really, his activities bordered on piracy. Passing vessels were looted and seized no matter what flag they sailed under. The Dutch were particularly hard-hit by Grenville and early in 1651, enraged at the interference to their mercantile interests, decided on direct measures.

Despite Charles' claim to power, at that time for the most part it was the Commonwealth government of Oliver Cromwell which held authority in England, recognising him only as 'King of the Scots'. Together with their new-found Dutch allies, the Commonwealth prepared for action against Grenville. Dutch Admiral

▸ **The stone steps** up to Star Castle. Over the entrance, the inscription reads: 'ER 1593'. To the left is a small alarm-bell tower. From an Edwardian postcard (AUTHOR'S COLLECTION).

Maarten Harpertszoon Tromp appeared off the islands during March, having taken the vigorous step of declaring war on them. Tromp's force of thirteen men-of-war was joined the following month by a British squadron under Admiral Robert Blake.

Grenville sought to placate the Dutch by returning prisoners, but couldn't give back their ships; he'd sold them. Blake, concerned Tromp might have territorial aspirations, insisted only Commonwealth forces would land on the Islands. Most of Grenville's force was based on St Mary's, but a small outpost occupied the Tresco castle; to secure a safe anchorage Blake decided to seize the smaller island first. He mounted his attack from the eastern side, landing by night. The Royalists fought on the beach, but after a sharp exchange were defeated.

Their castle was assaulted from landward. By then it had become known as Charles Castle, though the Prince is not thought to have visited during his stay. In command of the small garrison was Cornish Royalist William Edgcumb. The attacking troops quickly overran the castle's weak landside defences, and to prevent it falling into enemy hands Edgcumb resorted to blowing it up. He was assumed to have been killed in the blast but managed to make his escape to St Mary's, and thence to France. In a mighty twist to the tale, William later married the daughter of a Commonwealth general.

▲ **Tresco's Charles Castle** has had restorative work carried out, and today is well worth a walk to inspect. This is the castle's vulnerable landside rear (IMAGE BY KIND PERMISSION OF COLIN JACKSON).

▲ Cromwell's Castle was built after the English Civil War, to replace King Charles Castle. The ruins of both survive today, though the later fortification is much better positioned to defend Tresco's harbour of New Grimsby. The prominent artillery platform at the shoreline was added during the 1740s (Pete London).

Having taken Tresco and its neighbour Bryher, Blake turned to St Mary's and ordered a bombardment of Star Castle, as well as the other Royalist positions, and their ships. Trapped, Grenville met with Blake to negotiate a peace settlement, though at first talks stalled. But under Blake's merciful terms and as their supplies and ammunition dwindled, on 23 May the Royalist force surrendered. By June, the Islands' fortifications were in the hands of Commonwealth troops.

Later that year, the victors began building a replacement for Charles Castle, better positioned to defend New Grimsby's anchorage. Not least of their worries was whether the Dutch might one day revisit and seize control of the Islands. Accordingly the fortification known as Cromwell's Castle took shape, sited on a tiny promontory near the water's edge just south of Charles Castle.

Around forty-five feet in diameter and just under sixty feet tall, the circular castle mounted its cannon on a platform at the top of the tower, firing through six gun-ports positioned equidistantly around its circumference; the occupants were able to fire at targets on the water, but also to the land side if necessary. Below were three storeys providing the garrison's living quarters, an ammunition store and a guardroom, with access via a circular stone staircase. Cromwell's Castle was completed in 1652, its walls twelve feet thick. A garrison of twenty arrived, but the Dutch never returned.

Up to Date

After the 1650s no more castles were built in Cornwall or the Isles of Scilly. Other types of fortifications appeared, but not akin to the great constructions of former times. As gunpowder and artillery were developed and became more destructive, the vulnerability of castles grew. Finally, even the mightiest of castles were unable to resist cannon fire for long, their lofty stone walls enticing and exposed targets for enemy fire. As castles declined, instead the use grew of low artillery forts and emplacements.

But not all the Cornish castles were abandoned. After the Civil War Falmouth's castles continued in service, though they were adapted and added to in the face of changing times and requirements. Toward the end of the 1600s, at a time of French support for the Jacobite cause, Pendennis received a new gatehouse and guard barracks. Over the 1730s some of its ancient cannon were replaced. Additional gun batteries appeared during Napoleonic times; the mid-1800s and late 1880s saw further rearmament programmes. During the First World War Pendennis formed part of a system of coastal batteries protecting Falmouth. After a skeleton existence between the wars, the early 1940s saw new guns arrive. Through all the changes around it, Henry VIII's original castle remained. Finally though, in 1956 the military

▲ **Restormel Castle's keep** today. The grounds provide a quiet sanctuary with stunning views, ideal for a peaceful day out (Pete London).

▲ Overgrown Trematon Castle seen in 1840, engraved from a drawing by Thomas Allom (AUTHOR'S COLLECTION).

moved out for good as the Ministry of Works took over Pendennis as an ancient monument.

Following its fall in the Civil War, on the Monarchy's restoration during 1660 St Mawes returned to the control of the Vyvyan family, but was subsequently sold and passed through a chain of owners; the office of Governor was abolished in 1849. The castle subsequently served as a military training establishment, and with Pendennis formed part of Falmouth's First World War coastal defence scheme. In 1920 St Mawes passed to the Commissioner of Works as an Ancient Monument. However, the army reappeared during 1939, and the castle was rearmed to help counter the German E-boat threat. But by 1956, like its cousin across the water, St Mawes had been taken over by the Ministry of Works.

The third of Henry VIII's Cornish chain, St Catherine's Castle at Fowey, had played no part in the Civil War. The town had been seized by Royalist forces during 1644, and in March 1646 had surrendered to General Fairfax. But though it lay derelict throughout the war, subsequently St Catherine's must have received attention; during 1667, manned by seamen, a Dutch fleet lurking offshore was kept at bay by furious cannon-fire. Around the 1730s an additional artillery bastion appeared, and during the Crimean War a further battery of two guns was built below the castle. Later the site was used for artillery practice and in the Second World War acted as a battery and observation post.

Cornwall's medieval castles also had some life left in them. By the mid-seventeenth century the only habitable part of Launceston Castle was its northern gatehouse, though the courtyard continued to house the town's gaol. During the 1760s and '70s the gatehouse was partly dismantled, to donate stone to a new house being constructed across the road. Public hangings at Launceston continued until around 1821. In 1838 though, new assizes opened for business at Bodmin; two years later Launceston's gaol finally closed. The castle came into the hands of the Duke of Northumberland, who had its bailey and surrounding area landscaped into a public park. During the Second World War the site housed a temporary American military hospital but in 1951 Launceston was leased to the Ministry of Works.

Restormel's ruins also became gardens. During the mid-eighteenth century its overgrown walls were incorporated in a sprawling landscape contrived by Thomas Jones, a lawyer who'd retired nearby. During 1846, while travelling in the Duchy, Queen Victoria called at Restormel; in 1865 her eldest son Edward Duke of

▲ Tourists at Tintagel, 1950s-style. Behind our explorers are the medieval island courtyard and the hall, ahead of them Dark-Age ruins (AUTHOR'S COLLECTION).

Cornwall visited. Finally, during 1925 the Duchy of Cornwall gave custody of Restormel to the Ministry of Works. Terribly overgrown by then, over the following years the foliage was removed, stonework stabilised.

To the east, crumbling Trematon Castle provided a useful if informal source of recycled building material, until the arrival of Benjamin Tucker in 1807. During the following year Tucker became Surveyor General to the Duchy of Cornwall. He leased the castle from the Duchy, and decided to build a house for himself within its bailey. To enjoy the views across the Tamar and the Lynher he dismantled chunks of the castle's curtain wall, which was unpopular among historians and antiquarians; but had Trematon been left, the locals would probably have continued their own inroads.

Building work went on for at least fifteen years, the bill over six thousand pounds, but the result was a beautiful two-storey Regency mansion in a unique setting. The grand house stayed in the Tucker family for generations but in 1964 was occupied by life peer Lord Caradon, formerly Sir Hugh Foot, and his wife Sylvia, who lived there for two decades.

Meanwhile in the west, during 1659 the lease to St Michael's Mount had been bought from the Bassett family by Colonel John St Aubyn of Clowance. Since then, the Mount has led a generally peaceful existence, though during the Napoleonic Wars a brief exchange of fire took place with a passing French ship. The St Aubyn family has overseen its gradual transformation from a modest seventeenth-century castle to the current spectacular landmark. During 1727 its harbour was rebuilt, which helped support export of tin and copper; gradually too, adjacent houses appeared. Queen Victoria visited the Mount in 1846, and during the 1870s the substantial south-east wing was added.

Tintagel Castle took a very different turn. During Victorian times the legend of King Arthur began to appear in romantic writing, linked to the site of the castle. Alfred Lord Tennyson visited; his Idylls of the King, the first of which appeared in 1856, and Morte d'Arthur, told the stories of Arthur, his knights, Guinevere and the traitor Mordred, in which Tintagel became Arthur's birthplace. Dickens and Thackeray also wrote on Arthurian Tintagel. During 1863 Robert S Hawker, Vicar of Morwenstow, composed his greatest poem (though not his best-known work) The Quest of the Sangraal, a mixture of religious and Arthurian themes.

As fascination with the stories grew, Tintagel began its makeover into a tourist destination. The office of Castle Constable was revived, a castle guide appeared, and work began to spruce up the ruins. Around the turn of the century the adjacent village of Trevena changed its name to Tintagel. Visiting the castle was made easier once the railway at nearby Camelford opened in 1893. During 1929, the Duchy of Cornwall gave over care of Tintagel to the Ministry of Works. Several archaeological investigations have since taken place to uncover as much accurate history of the site as possible, an aspiration considerably at odds with the Arthurian tales peddled by the tourist trade.

On the Isles of Scilly, Star Castle served as a prison under both the Commonwealth and then Charles II. By 1669 a garrison of two hundred men were stationed there; later, the castle was used as the Governor's residence. During the first half of the eighteenth century The Hugh was reinforced, and became known as The Garrison; its curtain wall was rebuilt and extended around most of the headland. The Garrison's gate was reconstructed and three large artillery bastions appeared at Morning Point, south of Steval Point, and at Woolpack Point, covering the harbour approaches. King Charles' Battery and Newman's Battery defended the northern side. In the 1890s three further batteries were built, and during both World Wars The Garrison was a defended site.

Though Tresco's Charles Castle remained ruined, during the 1740s its neighbour benefited from refurbishment by Abraham Tovey, Master Gunner. A gun platform was constructed on Cromwell Castle's seaward side; a new guardhouse and entrance also appeared. The platform received nine-pounder cannon and the tower platform four-pounders, but after Napoleonic times gradually the castle fell into disuse.

▲ **A Victorian image** of Tintagel, its small bay hosting a sailing ship. To the left, ruins of the two landside baileys and on the peninsula the great hall and courtyard (AUTHOR'S COLLECTION).

Castles Today

Today at Cornwall's castle sites there's much to see. Among the earliest fortifications perhaps Neolithic Carn Brea is the most spectacular, its elevated position and extraordinary scoured rock formations lending an air of fantasy and unreality. Two particularly impressive Iron Age hillforts are Chûn Castle and St Columb Major's Castle-an-Dinas, not just for their substantial remains but again because of the views they command. Trevelgue Head is the easiest cliff castle to reach, but for those who enjoy a tramp there are plenty of others to choose from. Gurnards Head and Treryn Dinas are among the most attractive and while visiting the latter you can take in the well-known Logan Rock.

Restormel Castle's great stone shell keep is one of the best examples in Britain. Its original drawbridge has long been replaced by a solid walkway while inside, substantial signs of the rooms are still visible. The well also survives, together with part of the truly enormous kitchen fireplace and chimney. Around the top of the keep, the wall-walk is open to the public. Each spring the banks of Restormel's moat become a sea of daffodils and bluebells; set in rolling countryside, the spot provides a beautiful place for picnicking.

Launceston's lofty motte too has presence; the ascent to the top of its interior tower is well worth making. Much work has taken place at Launceston, not least to repair damage caused by the creation of the Duke of Northumberland's park, which paid scant regard to the site's archaeological importance. In the former bailey, ruins of various buildings have been recovered and stabilised including the great hall and at the perimeter, parts of the gatehouses and curtain wall. Today within the bustling town, the park is a peaceful oasis. Both Launceston and Restormel Castles are open to the public between March and October.

Tintagel is open for business throughout the year and is worth a visit for the views alone, a spectacular vista along cliffs which even on a sunny summer's day can convey a dark moodiness. Over the centuries landslips have caused further parts of the castle to fall into the sea, particularly from the two mainland baileys. The remaining ruins though, Dark Age and medieval, have been well-preserved.

Of Trematon Castle, the grand gatehouse and ovoid shell survive, while despite Benjamin Tucker's labours a large part of the surrounding curtain wall is more-or-less intact. In places the battlements are almost complete. Sadly Trematon is off-limits to viewing, though it can be seen from the River Lynher below, or from the nearby road.

Pendennis and St Mawes are open year-round, intact and sympathetically maintained. St Mawes now sits among beautiful, tranquil gardens, and from both

▲ **Keeping watch over** the Fowey estuary, the ruins of St Catherine's Castle are still with us today. On the far bank a bonfire lends atmosphere, the smoke of conflict and cannon (Pete London).

sites the views across the Carrick Roads are inspiring. At Fowey, St Catherine's Castle is reasonably complete and once again the setting is wonderful.

The best-known and most romantic of Cornwall's castles of course is St Michael's Mount. The St Aubyn family is still in residence, but both the castle and its exquisite gardens are open. Eighteenth-century seafront cottages, cobbled walkways and the grey granite harbour add to the feeling of stepping back in time, while at the waterfront the St Aubyn Arms still stands, though its licence to sell alcohol came to an end in 1902.

On the Isles of Scilly, Ennor Castle's stone keep survives only in places, together with some earthwork banks and a mound of rubble. During 1933 Star Castle opened as a hotel, in a ceremony at which the short-lived future King Edward VIII officiated, and since 1975 has been a Grade 1 Listed Building. Nearby, earthworks remain as originally thrown up during the Civil War, a rarity today since most were temporary, hurriedly-built structures.

▲ Cromwell's Castle seen from the eastern side. Its all-round gun-ports allowed firing against enemies on land, as well as at sea (IMAGE REPRODUCED BY KIND PERMISSION OF ANDREW ABBOTT).

Following its demise with the help of gunpowder, the ruins of Charles Castle have received some restorative reassembly. On the shoreline below, in better condition and sited in a far more effective military position, Cromwell's Castle still stands guard over Tresco's main anchorage. As a fortification though, it's no longer necessary; in April 1986 a formal peace treaty, carelessly overlooked in Dutch Admiral Tromp's time, was signed between the Isles of Scilly and the Netherlands. Finally, history's longest war at three hundred and thirty-five years, and the war with fewest casualties, was brought to a close.